CLARINET

101 MOST BEAUTIFUL SONGS

Available for
FLUTE, CLARINET, ALTO SAX, TENOR SAX, TRUMPET,
HORN, TROMBONE, VIOLIN, VIOLA, CELLO

ISBN 978-1-5400-4820-2

HAL•LEONARD®

Visit Hal Leonard Online at
www.halleonard.com

World headquarters, contact:
Hal Leonard
7777 West Bluemound Road
Milwaukee, WI 53213
Email: info@halleonard.com

In Europe, contact:
Hal Leonard Europe Limited
1 Red Place
London, W1K 6PL
Email: info@halleonardeurope.com

In Australia, contact:
Hal Leonard Australia Pty. Ltd.
4 Lentara Court
Cheltenham, Victoria, 3192 Australia
Email: info@halleonard.com.au

CONTENTS

ALWAYS

CLARINET

Words and Music by
IRVING BERLIN

ALWAYS ON MY MIND

Clarinet

Words and Music by WAYNE THOMPSON,
MARK JAMES and JOHNNY CHRISTOPHER

AND I LOVE HER

CLARINET

Words and Music by JOHN LENNON
and PAUL McCARTNEY

AND I LOVE YOU SO

Words and Music by
DON McLEAN

Clarinet

AND SO IT GOES

CLARINET

Words and Music by
BILLY JOEL

Slow Ballad, with much rubato

ANNIE'S SONG

CLARINET

Words and Music by
JOHN DENVER

ANYWHERE IS

CLARINET

Words and Music by ENYA,
NICKY RYAN and ROMA RYAN

D.S. al Coda

CODA

BEIN' GREEN

CLARINET

Words and Music by
JOE RAPOSO

BLACKBIRD

CLARINET

Words and Music by JOHN LENNON
and PAUL McCARTNEY

THE BOOK OF LOVE

CLARINET

Words and Music by
STEPHIN MERRITT

CODA

THE BOXER

CLARINET

Words and Music by
PAUL SIMON

Moderately, in 2

BRING HIM HOME
from LES MISÉRABLES

Clarinet

Music by CLAUDE-MICHEL SCHÖNBERG
Lyrics by HERBERT KRETZMER and ALAIN BOUBLIL

Moderately slow

BY THE TIME I GET TO PHOENIX

CLARINET

Words and Music by
JIMMY WEBB

CANDLE IN THE WIND

Clarinet

Words and Music by ELTON JOHN
and BERNIE TAUPIN

Slow 2

A CHILD IS BORN

CLARINET

By THAD JONES

(They Long to Be)
CLOSE TO YOU

Clarinet

Lyrics by HAL DAVID
Music by BURT BACHARACH

CITY OF STARS
from LA LA LAND

Clarinet

Music by JUSTIN HURWITZ
Lyrics by BENJ PASEK & JUSTIN PAUL

Slower

rit.

COME SUNDAY
from BLACK, BROWN & BEIGE

CLARINET

By DUKE ELLINGTON

CRAZY

CLARINET

Words and Music by
WILLIE NELSON

CRYING

CLARINET

Words and Music by ROY ORBISON
and JOE MELSON

Moderately slow, with feeling

DREAM A LITTLE DREAM OF ME

CLARINET

Words by GUS KAHN
Music by WILBUR SCHWANDT
and FABIAN ANDREE

DAUGHTERS

CLARINET

Words and Music by
JOHN MAYER

D.S. al Coda

CODA

EASY LIVING
Theme from the Paramount Picture EASY LIVING

Clarinet

Words and Music by LEO ROBIN
and RALPH RAINGER

ETERNAL FLAME

CLARINET

Words and Music by BILLY STEINBERG,
TOM KELLY and SUSANNA HOFFS

ETERNALLY

CLARINET

Words by GEOFFREY PARSONS
Music by CHARLES CHAPLIN

Slowly, with feeling

EVERY BREATH YOU TAKE

CLARINET

Music and Lyrics by
STING

(EVERYTHING I DO) I DO IT FOR YOU

from the Motion Picture ROBIN HOOD: PRINCE OF THIEVES

CLARINET

Written by MICHAEL KAMEN

FEELING GOOD

from THE ROAR OF THE GREASEPAINT – THE SMELL OF THE CROWD

Clarinet

Words and Music by LESLIE BRICUSSE
and ANTHONY NEWLEY

FOR ALL WE KNOW

Clarinet

Words by SAM M. LEWIS
Music by J. FRED COOTS

GABRIEL'S OBOE

from the Motion Picture THE MISSION

CLARINET

Words and Music by
ENNIO MORRICONE

Slowly, expressively

GOOD NIGHT

CLARINET

Words and Music by JOHN LENNON
and PAUL McCARTNEY

GOODNIGHT, SWEETHEART, GOODNIGHT
(Goodnight, It's Time to Go)

CLARINET

Words and Music by JAMES HUDSON
and CALVIN CARTER

HAVE I TOLD YOU LATELY

CLARINET

Words and Music by
VAN MORRISON

HELLO

CLARINET

Words and Music by
LIONEL RICHIE

Slow Ballad

HEAL THE WORLD

CLARINET

Words and Music by
MICHAEL JACKSON

Moderately slow

HERE, THERE AND EVERYWHERE

CLARINET

Words and Music by JOHN LENNON
and PAUL McCARTNEY

Moderately slow

HIGHLAND CATHEDRAL

CLARINET

By MICHAEL KORB
and ULRICH ROEVER

Stately March, in 2

I HAVE A DREAM
from MAMMA MIA!

Clarinet

Words and Music by BENNY ANDERSSON
and BJÖRN ULVAEUS

D.S. al Coda

CODA

I LEFT MY HEART IN SAN FRANCISCO

Clarinet

Words by DOUGLASS CROSS
Music by GEORGE CORY

I WILL

CLARINET

Words and Music by JOHN LENNON
and PAUL McCARTNEY

Moderately

I'LL BE AROUND

CLARINET

Words and Music by
ALEC WILDER

Slowly, with expression

I'LL BE SEEING YOU

from RIGHT THIS WAY

Clarinet

Written by IRVING KAHAL
and SAMMY FAIN

I'VE DREAMED OF YOU

CLARINET

Words and Music by ANN HAMPTON CALLAWAY
and ROLF LOVLAND

Moderately slow

53

Freely

IN MY ROOM

CLARINET

Words and Music by BRIAN WILSON
and GARY USHER

LA VIE EN ROSE
(Take Me to Your Heart Again)

Clarinet

Original French Lyrics by EDITH PIAF
Music by LUIGUY
English Lyrics by MACK DAVID

Slowly, with expression

JUST GIVE ME A REASON

Clarinet

Words and Music by ALECIA MOORE,
JEFF BHASKER and NATE RUESS

CODA

LADY IN RED

CLARINET

Words and Music by
CHRIS DeBURGH

LET IT BE ME
(Je t'appartiens)

Clarinet

English Words by MANN CURTIS
French Words by PIERRE DeLANOE
Music by GILBERT BECAUD

LOST IN YOUR EYES

CLARINET

Words and Music by
DEBORAH GIBSON

Moderately slow

LOVE ME TENDER

CLARINET

Words and Music by ELVIS PRESLEY
and VERA MATSON

LOVING YOU

Clarinet

Words and Music by JERRY LEIBER
and MIKE STOLLER

LULLABYE
(Goodnight, My Angel)

CLARINET

Words and Music by
BILLY JOEL

Rubato, gently

MIA & SEBASTIAN'S THEME

from LA LA LAND

CLARINET

Music by
JUSTIN HURWITZ

Moderately slow, expressively

MICHELLE

CLARINET

Words and Music by JOHN LENNON
and PAUL McCARTNEY

MONA LISA

from the Paramount Picture CAPTAIN CAREY, U.S.A.

CLARINET

Words and Music by JAY LIVINGSTON
and RAY EVANS

MY FOOLISH HEART

CLARINET

Words by NED WASHINGTON
Music by VICTOR YOUNG

Slowly and expressively

MY FUNNY VALENTINE

from BABES IN ARMS

Clarinet

Words by LORENZ HART
Music by RICHARD RODGERS

MY VALENTINE

CLARINET

Words and Music by
PAUL McCARTNEY

MY WAY

Clarinet

English Words by PAUL ANKA
Original French Words by GILLES THIBAULT
Music by JACQUES REVAUX and CLAUDE FRANCOIS

NANCY WITH THE LAUGHING FACE

CLARINET

Words by PHIL SILVERS
Music by JAMES VAN HEUSEN

Moderately

NATURE BOY

CLARINET

Words and Music by
EDEN AHBEZ

NEVER ENOUGH

from THE GREATEST SHOWMAN

Clarinet

Words and Music by BENJ PASEK
and JUSTIN PAUL

A NIGHTINGALE SANG IN BERKELEY SQUARE

CLARINET

Lyric by ERIC MASCHWITZ
Music by MANNING SHERWIN

PERFECT

CLARINET

Words and Music by
ED SHEERAN

PHOTOGRAPH

CLARINET

Words and Music by ED SHEERAN,
JOHNNY McDAID, MARTIN PETER HARRINGTON
and TOM LEONARD

Moderately

THE PLACE WHERE LOST THINGS GO

from MARY POPPINS RETURNS

CLARINET

Music by MARC SHAIMAN
Lyrics by SCOTT WITTMAN and MARC SHAIMAN

RAINY DAYS AND MONDAYS

Lyrics by PAUL WILLIAMS
Music by ROGER NICHOLS

Clarinet

RELEASE ME

CLARINET

Words and Music by ROBERT YOUNT,
EDDIE MILLER and DUB WILLIAMS

REWRITE THE STARS

from THE GREATEST SHOWMAN

Clarinet

Words and Music by BENJ PASEK
and JUSTIN PAUL

Moderately fast

SAILING

CLARINET

Words and Music by
CHRISTOPHER CROSS

SCARBOROUGH FAIR/CANTICLE

CLARINET

Arrangement and Original Counter Melody by
PAUL SIMON and ARTHUR GARFUNKEL

SHALLOW

from A STAR IS BORN

Clarinet

Words and Music by STEFANI GERMANOTTA,
MARK RONSON, ANDREW WYATT
and ANTHONY ROSSOMANDO

SINCE I DON'T HAVE YOU

Clarinet

Words and Music by JAMES BEAUMONT,
JANET VOGEL, JOSEPH VERSCHAREN,
WALTER LESTER, LENNIE MARTIN,
JOSEPH ROCK and JOHN TAYLOR

Slowly, with a strong, rockin' beat

SHE'S ALWAYS A WOMAN

CLARINET

Words and Music by
BILLY JOEL

SMILE
Theme from MODERN TIMES

CLARINET

Words by JOHN TURNER and GEOFFREY PARSONS
Music by CHARLES CHAPLIN

SMOKE GETS IN YOUR EYES
from ROBERTA

Clarinet

Words by OTTO HARBACH
Music by JEROME KERN

SOMETHING WONDERFUL
from THE KING AND I

Clarinet

Lyrics by OSCAR HAMMERSTEIN II
Music by RICHARD RODGERS

Moderately

SOMEWHERE

from WEST SIDE STORY

Clarinet

Lyrics by STEPHEN SONDHEIM
Music by LEONARD BERNSTEIN

THE SOUND OF SILENCE

CLARINET

Words and Music by
PAUL SIMON

STARDUST

Clarinet

Words by MITCHELL PARISH
Music by HOAGY CARMICHAEL

STRANGERS IN THE NIGHT

adapted from A MAN COULD GET KILLED

Clarinet

Words by CHARLES SINGLETON
and EDDIE SNYDER
Music by BERT KAEMPFERT

Moderately slow

SWAY
(Quien será)

CLARINET

English Words by NORMAN GIMBEL
Spanish Words and Music by PABLO BELTRÁN RUIZ
and LUIS DEMETRIO TRACONIS MOLINA

Moderately

TENNESSEE WALTZ

Clarinet

Words and Music by REDD STEWART
and PEE WEE KING

(THERE IS) NO GREATER LOVE

Clarinet

Words by MARTY SYMES
Music by ISHAM JONES

With emotion

THEY SAY IT'S WONDERFUL

from the Stage Production ANNIE GET YOUR GUN

CLARINET

Words and Music by
IRVING BERLIN

THREE TIMES A LADY

CLARINET

Words and Music by
LIONEL RICHIE

TIME TO SAY GOODBYE

Clarinet

Words by LUCIO QUARANTOTTO
and FRANK PETERSON
Music by FRANCESCO SARTORI

TRUE COLORS

CLARINET

Words and Music by BILLY STEINBERG
and TOM KELLY

TRULY

CLARINET

Words and Music by
LIONEL RICHIE

UNEXPECTED SONG
from SONG & DANCE

CLARINET

Music by ANDREW LLOYD WEBBER
Lyrics by DON BLACK

WE'VE ONLY JUST BEGUN

Clarinet

Words and Music by ROGER NICHOLS
and PAUL WILLIAMS

WE'VE GOT TONIGHT

CLARINET

Words and Music by
BOB SEGER

WHAT A WONDERFUL WORLD

Clarinet

Words and Music by GEORGE DAVID WEISS
and BOB THIELE

WONDERFUL TONIGHT

CLARINET

Words and Music by
ERIC CLAPTON

YESTER-ME, YESTER-YOU, YESTERDAY

Words by RON MILLER
Music by BRYAN WELLS

CLARINET

Moderately

YESTERDAY ONCE MORE

Clarinet

Words and Music by JOHN BETTIS
and RICHARD CARPENTER

YESTERDAY, WHEN I WAS YOUNG
(Hier Encore)

CLARINET

English Lyric by HERBERT KRETZMER
Original French Text and Music by CHARLES AZNAVOUR

YOU ARE THE SUNSHINE OF MY LIFE

Clarinet

Words and Music by
STEVIE WONDER

Moderately

YOU'RE THE INSPIRATION

CLARINET

Words and Music by PETER CETERA
and DAVID FOSTER

YOUNG AT HEART

from YOUNG AT HEART

Clarinet

Words by CAROLYN LEIGH
Music by JOHNNY RICHARDS

YOUR SONG

Clarinet

Words and Music by ELTON JOHN
and BERNIE TAUPIN